Chicken by Charlie

First published in 2013 by Grass Roots Press

Grass Roots Press gratefully acknowledges the financial support for its publishing programs provided by the following agencies: the Government of Canada through the Canada Book Fund and the Government of Alberta through the Alberta Foundation for the Arts.

Library and Archives Canada Cataloguing in Publication

Reiff, Tana
        Chicken by Charlie / Tana Reiff. — Rev. ed.

(Pathfinders)
Previous title: Chicken by Che.
ISBN 978–1–927499–66–5

        1. Readers (Adult). 2. Readers for new literates.
I. Reiff, Tana. Chicken by Che. II. Title. III. Series:
Pathfinders (Edmonton, Alta.)

PE1127.W65R438 2013   428.6'2   C2012–906775–X

Cover image: © Tanya Constantine/Blend Images/Corbis

Printed and bound in Canada.

Chicken by Charlie
Tana Reiff

Grass Roots Press

Chapter 1

The chicken
tasted just right.
The vegetables
were fresh and hot.
Every bit of food
looked just right too.
Charlie, the chef,
was very pleased.
She handed the plate
to the server.
Out it sailed
into the sea of tables.
There was a crowd
this large
every night.

The restaurant
was the finest around.
The menu
had dishes

from around the world.
Everything about this place
was fancy,
not only the food.

But Charlie
was not as happy
as the people
she cooked for.
She dreamed of cooking
for people like her,
in her part of town.
She wanted
to cook chicken
her own way.
She wanted
to fry it
with her own blend
of spices.
She wanted
to cook chicken
the way she cooked
at home,
for her family.

Charlie was thinking
about all this
as she rushed
around the busy kitchen.

Just then,
one of the servers
burst into the kitchen.
"Charlie, do you have
a minute?"
he asked.
"The man at Table 5
wants to talk to you."

"One minute!"
Charlie called out.
"Watch this pan, please,"
she asked one of the cooks.
She wiped
her hot face.
Out she flew
into the dining room.

"Most delicious chicken
I ever ate!"

said the man at Table 5.
"Nothing short of perfect!"

"Why, thank you!"
smiled Charlie.
"I am so happy
to hear that."

"What is your name?"

"Charlene,
but everyone
calls me Charlie."

"Charlie, you are
a fine chef,"
said the man.
"You should open
your own restaurant."

Charlie thought
that this man
was reading her mind.
Having her own restaurant

was always on her mind.
It was a dream
that had become part of her.
She didn't know
what to say.
She didn't want
to talk about her dream
right here, right now.

So she said,
"I'm glad
you enjoyed your dinner."
The man
put out his hand.
Charlie wiped hers
on a clean part
of her apron
and shook his hand.

"Thank you, sir,"
she said.
"I'll think about
what you said.
"Very nice meeting you."

Chapter 2

At home,
Charlie thought about
her dream.
She knew
what she wanted
in a restaurant.
Her own restaurant
would not be fancy.
The food
would not cost much.
The main dish
would be chicken.
She knew
what she would call
her restaurant.
Chicken by Charlie,
of course.

Charlie even knew
the right spot
for the restaurant.

She had her eye
on an empty space
in her part of town.
It was at the corner
of Second and Green Streets.

Chicken by Charlie
would be open
for lunch and dinner.
There would be
two work shifts.
For each shift,
Charlie would need
two counter people
and one cleanup person.
There would be
no table service.
So she would not need
to hire servers.
She would do
all the cooking herself.

Chicken by Charlie
would have
the best chicken around.

People would come
from near and far.
And then
they would come back
for more.

Charlie's husband, Ben,
and their children
walked in.

"Hey, my sunny girl!"
said Ben
as he kissed Charlie.
Ben knew
about her dream.
He didn't know how far
the dream had come.

"What do you think?"
Charlie asked
after telling Ben
about her big ideas.

Their three children
loved the idea.

"You could bring chicken home!
We could eat chicken
every day!"
they squealed.

But Ben
was not so fired up.
"The restaurant business
is not easy,"
he said.
"It's long hours.
You have to do
every little thing
by the book.
If you mess up,
you're out of business.
You never know
what could go wrong.
You might not
make money
for a long time.
You do this, Charlie,
if you want to.
I'm behind you.

But we had better
put away some money—
now, while we can."

"It will work,"
said Charlie.
"I know
I can make it work.
And my restaurant
will make money
sooner than you think.
Just you wait!"

Chapter 3

To start a restaurant,
Charlie would need
a business loan.
And a business plan,
which had been
in her mind
for a long time.
Now all she had to do
was put the plan together.
From working
as a chef,
she knew
what things cost.
What she didn't know,
she looked up online.
She added up
how much money
she would need.
Then she took her plan
to the bank.

"Mr. Glass will see you,"
said the woman
at the bank.
She showed Charlie
to his office.

Charlie reached out
to shake his hand.
Then she stopped cold.
She knew this face.
"Aren't you the man
from the restaurant?
The one who told me
I should open
my own restaurant?"

"I sure am!"
said Mr. Glass.
"Great to see you!"

Charlie showed him
her business plan.
Mr. Glass said
it looked very clear.

He asked questions.
"Are there
no chain restaurants
near Second and Green?
No other chicken
to go up against?"

"Not a one,"
said Charlie.
"It's a busy corner.
Lots of people walk by
all the time.
That's why
it's the perfect place
for my restaurant."

Mr. Glass
filled out a form
on his computer.
He told her
there was a good chance
of getting a loan
for a new business
in her part of town.

Then Charlie
waited to hear
from the bank.
She waited
and waited.
She waited
for four weeks.
It was
a long four weeks.

At last,
Mr. Glass called.
"I'm happy to tell you
your loan
has come through,"
he said.

"Glad I could
put my money
where my mouth is."

Charlie's face
turned into one big smile.
She felt her dream
coming to life.

The next step
was to leave her job.
Everyone at the restaurant
was very sorry
to see her go.
Even Sal, the boss.
"I'm going to miss you,"
he said with a hug.
"If you need anything,
let me know."

Chapter 4

Charlie began working
on her chicken recipe.
She made little changes
along the way.
Her kids
had wanted chicken
every day.
They were getting it.
Charlie's chicken recipe
was getting better
every day too.

She wanted to rent
the building
at Second and Green.
But first,
she had to get
a long list of permits.

Then she signed a lease
and hired a contractor.

Charlie worked with him
to make changes
to the building.
New walls and floors.
A big kitchen
with a good work flow.
A little cold room
in the back.
And every last thing—
inside and outside,
up and down—
had to be done
by the rules.

Then Charlie went
on a dream shopping trip.
To her,
a restaurant supply store
was a theme park.
The place was packed
with great stuff.
She picked out
yellow tables and chairs.
She bought
plates and cups.

She ordered
printed napkins
and caps
and aprons
and boxes.
She found
the deep fryer
she wanted.
She chose
all the kitchen gear
she would need.
She was in heaven.

Then it was time
to hire staff.
She put
a HELP WANTED sign
in the window.
She posted online.
Almost 200 people
applied for the jobs.
Charlie could pick
only six.

Chapter 5

The day
of the grand opening
was very grand.
It was
a sunny day,
and hundreds of people
showed up.
Drinks were free that day,
and the food
almost ran out.
Charlie peeked out
from the kitchen
and saw a sea
of happy faces.
The grand opening
turned into a grand party.

"Delicious chicken!"
Charlie heard
one person after another

say as they left.
"We'll be back!"

Many of them
did come back.
Those first few weeks
were very busy.
But Charlie missed
most of the fun.
She was in the kitchen,
over a hot deep fryer.
She could hardly keep up.
Sometimes people
had to wait
to get their food.
Some of them
got tired of waiting
and left.

One day
the restaurant
was having
a big rush.
A line of people

ran all the way
out the front door.

All of a sudden,
the power went out.
The lights went dark.
In the kitchen,
everything stopped.

Charlie came out
to talk to the people.
"I'm so sorry,"
she said.
"The power is out.
We can't cook."

She wrote out
free drink coupons
on napkins.
"Please come back soon!"
Charlie told everyone.
"Come back and get
your free drink!"

The power came back
an hour later.
By then,
there was no one left
to cook for.

Charlie lost
a lot of money
that day.
It made her sick.
"If something bad
can happen,
it will,"
she told Ben that night.

"Where did
my sunny girl go?"
Ben wanted to know.

"She'll be back,"
said Charlie.
"Just one bad day."

Chapter 6

People did come back
to Chicken by Charlie.
They could not stay away
from that delicious chicken.
"I just hope
nothing else goes wrong,"
Charlie said to herself.

But only a week later
something else went wrong.
Very wrong.
It was
near closing time.
Charlie was in the kitchen
getting ready
to lock up
for the night.
The staff
was cleaning up.
A few people

were sitting at tables
eating chicken.
Charlie was running
on three hours of sleep.
She was about to fall over.

Just then,
two men came in.
They wore ski masks.
Only four eyes
and two mouths
showed through the masks.

"Put your hands up!"
they shouted.
"That means everyone!"

Charlie came out
from the kitchen.
"What's going on here?"
she asked.

"Hands in the air!"
the men shouted at her.

They waved guns
across the air,
from person to person.

"Now hand over
all your money!"
One by one,
the people handed over
their money.

Charlie opened
the cash drawer.
She handed over the money
without a word.

"Now turn around!"
the men ordered.
"Everyone! Into the back!"

The two men
spotted the cold room.
They stuffed everyone
into the little space.
They slammed the door shut

and turned the lock.
Then they took off
with the money.
They grabbed
a box of chicken
on the way out.

At 1:00 a.m.
the cops
drove by,
as they did every night.
They saw
that the lights
in the restaurant
were still on.
But they saw
no people inside.

The front door
was not locked.
So they went in.
They found
all the people,
stuffed like canned fish,

in the cold room.
The robbers
were long gone
with the money.
Charlie filed
a police report,
then went home.

Chapter 7

After the robbery,
business was slow.
People heard
what had happened
and stayed away.
Three of Charlie's workers
never came back.

Very little money
was coming in.
A week later,
a loan payment
was due.
Charlie did not
have enough money
to pay the bank.
She had only enough
to pay the workers.

She called
a staff meeting.

"How can we
get people
to come back?"
she asked.

A guy named Levi
had an idea.
"We could have
a game,"
he said.
"People could play
for free.
Once a week
we could
draw a name.
That person
will win
a free chicken dinner
for four."

The whole staff
liked the idea.
So did Charlie.

"I hope this helps,"
she said.
"I want to hire people.
I don't want
to lay off people."

Charlie filed a form
to run the game.
There were rules
about such games.
She just had to
follow the rules.

And so
the game began.
It was called
A Game of Chicken.
It wasn't really
a game of chicken,
just a catchy name.

Chapter 8

Levi made
a big sign
for the window:
PLAY A GAME OF CHICKEN!
Anyone walking by
Chicken by Charlie
couldn't miss it.
Those big letters
caught people's eyes,
and in they came
to play the game.

The first winner
was a woman
with three kids,
just like Charlie.
Charlie was glad
the woman had won.
This family
really needed
a free chicken dinner.

And it was perfect.
Four people
in the family.
Four free dinners.

Charlie also was glad
for the jump in business.
Now she had
enough money
to pay the bank.
Things were looking up.

The next week
another worker quit.
He said it was because
he didn't like
working weekends.

Then someone else quit.
She was going
to have a baby.
The smell of chicken
made her sick.

Another worker
took off
over the holidays.

The workers
who stayed on
got really busy.
They started
making mistakes.
A customer
found a bug
in her food.
She called
the board of health.

The board of health
came to check things out.
They looked
at every little thing
in the restaurant.
They found no bugs.
Everything checked out.
But they told Charlie
to be more careful.

Next time,
if anything was wrong,
she would have to
pay a fine.

And then one day,
Charlie was counting money
to take to the bank.
The count
seemed short.
The busy lunch
should have brought in
more cash.

She counted again.
It was much less
than on any other day.
No question,
the cash was short.

She took a look
at how much
had been paid
with cards.

Card payments
added up
to about the same
as any other day.

What was going on?
That question
stayed in Charlie's mind
as she walked
to the bank.
And it stayed
on her mind
all night long.

Chapter 9

Where was
the missing money?
Charlie had no idea.
She didn't say anything
to her staff.
But she did
keep her eyes open.

During the next months,
workers came and went.
Charlie had to hire
new people
again and again.

One night
the deep fryer
caught on fire.
Insurance paid
to fix it.
But Charlie lost money

while the deep fryer
was down.

The fire
had messed up
the kitchen too.
"I'll stay late
and clean it up,"
Levi said.
"Don't pay me
for that time.
I want to help.
We are all
in this together."

"That is good of you,"
Charlie told him.
She was so busy,
and then had three kids
at home.
She needed
all the help
she could get.

Levi did
a great job.
The kitchen
looked like new.
Maybe even better
than new.

When Charlie saw
what Levi had done,
she made up her mind.
It was time
to move Levi up.

"Levi," she said.
"I think I need
an assistant manager.
How about it?
I'll give you
a nice raise."

Charlie did not want
Levi to leave,
like the others had.

Chapter 10

For Charlie's birthday,
Ben cooked her
a special dinner.
So Charlie
left the restaurant
early that day
to have dinner
with her family.
She left Levi
in charge.

After dinner
she went back
to the restaurant
to close up.
She walked up
to the door.
All the workers
had gone home.
Only Levi
was still there.

He did not
see her coming.

Then Charlie saw
something
she wished
she wasn't seeing.
Levi was taking money
out of the cash drawer.

Charlie went inside.
"What are you doing?"
she asked Levi.

Levi looked up.
His mouth
dropped open.
He just stood there.

"Are you
stealing money?"
Charlie asked him.
"You?
Really?"

"Please, Charlie,"
begged Levi.
"I'm sorry.
I'll never do it again."

"Levi, Levi,"
cried Charlie.
"You were
my best worker.
My assistant manager.
Now I can never
trust you again.
I must
let you go."

"I understand,"
said Levi,
his head down.
"I'm so sorry."

"Did you ever
steal from me before?"
Charlie wanted to know.

Levi's head
dropped even more.
"I can't lie to you,"
he said.
"I took some money
a few weeks ago."

"I knew
the cash was short
one day,"
said Charlie.
"I never dreamed
you took it!
You have really
let me down."

Levi took off
his cap and apron.
He laid them
on a table.

"You go now,"
Charlie said.
"But someday
I want that money back."

Levi walked out,
still looking down.

Charlie's heart
was broken.
She had had
such high hopes for Levi.
Now he was gone,
and so was the money.

Chapter 11

Charlie went home.
She was still upset
about Levi.
She went
over and over things
in her head.
How could she have missed
what was going on?

She made herself
a cup of tea
and sat down
at her kitchen table.

She made a list.
Levi was not
the only problem.
She wrote down
all the problems
at the restaurant.

But she didn't know
how to fix them.

Then she remembered
her old boss, Sal.
"If you need anything,
let me know,"
he had told her.

So she went
to see Sal.
She needed his help.
She needed
to pick his brains
about how to run
her restaurant.

"How's it going?"
Sal asked Charlie.

"Sal, I need your help,"
said Charlie.
"Tell me all you know
about running a
restaurant."

"It's hard, isn't it?"
he said.
He rubbed his chin
and looked up.
"Where should I begin?"

"At the beginning,"
Charlie said.

Sal was full of
how-to ideas.
How to get the word out
without spending
much money.
How to hire good staff.
How to train them.
And how to
keep them happy
so they don't leave.
"Be the kind of boss
you would want
to work for,"
said Sal.

"Happy staff
make happy customers."

"Do you taste the food?
he went on.
"And who takes care
of the front
when you're in the back
cooking all the time?"

"I had an assistant manager,"
said Charlie.
"But he was stealing.
I had to let him go."

"It's a small restaurant,"
said Sal.
"Why do you need
an assistant?"

Sal was giving Charlie
a lot to think about.

"You are a great cook,"
he said.
"And you're strong.
You have a dream
and you won't let it die.
But these things
are not enough."

"You're right,"
said Charlie.
"I need
to make some changes.
For one thing,
I need to hire
a good cook."

"I didn't say that,"
Sal laughed.

"You made me see it
for myself,"
Charlie smiled.
"I need to be
closer to the customers.

But I don't have money
to hire a cook."

"Not enough money
is the number one reason
a business fails,"
said Sal.
"You might need
another loan."

Chapter 12

The next day
Charlie went
to see Mr. Glass
at the bank.

"You're asking
for more money?"
Mr. Glass asked.
"You're not in
over your head,
are you?"

"I need
to hire a cook,"
Charlie told him.
"I need time to do
other things
at the restaurant.
And I need
to spend some money
to get the word out."

"Let's back up,
said Mr. Glass.
"Have you thought about
giving up the restaurant?
Maybe you should get out
before you lose it all."

"No!" said Charlie.
"Please give me
one more chance.
I'm learning
as I go.
Every time
something goes wrong,
I learn from it.
I got some good ideas
from my old boss.
I'll build up
this business.
Just watch me.
But I need money
to do it."

Mr. Glass said nothing
for a full minute.

He looked
at some numbers
on his computer.
Then he looked
at Charlie.

"I believe in you,"
he told her.
"We can lend you
a little more money.
But that's it.
No more.
This is the last loan
you'll get from this bank."

Chapter 13

A young man
named Pedro
showed up one day.
He was looking
for a job.
He had come in
as a customer
many times.

"I've worked
in restaurants,"
he told Charlie.
"But never as a cook.
Cooking is my dream!
And Chicken by Charlie
is the best!"

"Why should I hire you?"
Charlie asked Pedro.

"I love to cook
and I work hard,"
Pedro began.
"What I don't know,
you can teach me.
I'm a fast learner.
And I have big ideas
for building the business!"

"Give me one,"
Charlie asked Pedro.

"I can dress up
like a chicken.
I can be outside
getting people
to come inside!"

Pedro went on and on.
He didn't come up for air.
After Big Idea number ten,
Charlie stopped him.
"Let's see
what you can do,"
she said.

She took Pedro
back to the kitchen.
She showed him
the steps to perfect chicken.
"Put on this apron,"
she said.
"It's your turn.
Make me some chicken."

Once Pedro got started,
he didn't want to stop.

"Okay! Okay!"
said Charlie.
"Let me taste."

Pedro's chicken
was perfect.

Charlie clapped her hands.
"You're hired!"
she said.
"I need a cook
right away.
When can you start?"

"Right away!"
Pedro said.

"Then keep your apron on!"
said Charlie.
"Now tell me.
Why are you
so full of ideas?"

"Because I believe
in Chicken by Charlie!"
said Pedro.
"I grew up here.
We never had
a good chicken restaurant.
Hard to believe,
but true.
And you saw that.
Now we have
Chicken by Charlie!"

"Why should I
believe in *you*?"
Charlie asked Pedro.

"Because I'm real,"
said Pedro.
"Talk to anyone
who knows me.
They will tell you.
I say what I mean
and do what I say.
I work hard.
I want
to learn everything!
Someday I want
my own restaurant."

"You sound like me,"
Charlie laughed.

"One more idea,"
said Pedro.
"We need to sell
burgers here too.
Believe it or not,
not everyone likes
chicken."

Chapter 14

In no time at all,
Pedro became
Charlie's best worker.
He cooked chicken
as if Charlie
had cooked it herself.
He did
whatever needed to be done.
With a smile.

Charlie tried out
Pedro's ideas.
She made
a silly chicken costume
out of real feathers.
Pedro put on the costume,
with yellow rubber gloves
over his feet.
He passed out coupons,
up and down the street,

clucking like a chicken.
That young man
never ran out
of steam.

Charlie cooked
while Pedro clucked.
Someone had to feed
all the new customers
Pedro the chicken
pulled in.

And Charlie
added burgers
to the menu.
Pedro got a kick
out of flipping burgers,
even if a few of them
fell on the floor.
And ended up
in the garbage.

Of course,
there were still

some problems.
Charlie still spent
most of her waking hours
at the restaurant
or around town
making deals
to sell more chicken.
But Ben's "sunny girl"
was sunny again
almost all the time.

Mr. Glass and the bank
were pleased.
Charlie kept the money
coming in.
Her loan payment
was on time
every month.
She even started
paying herself.

But Mr. Glass
was wrong
about one thing.

The second loan
was not the last.
Two years later
the bank
gave Charlie
a third loan.
She opened
another Chicken by Charlie
in another part of town.
Pedro helped her run it.

"Someday I'll have
ten restaurants!"
Charlie told Ben.

"One at a time!"
Ben laughed.

And so,
Chicken by Charlie
turned out to be
a dream come true.
It was everything
Charlie had hoped for.

And much more.
Sometimes the sailing
was not so smooth.
But the more money
Charlie made,
the better the chicken tasted.

Pathfinders

If you enjoyed this book, you will enjoy these other Pathfinders titles by Tana Reiff.